ALSO BY JUDITH VIORST

POEMS

The Village Square
It's Hard to Be Hip Over Thirty and Other Tragedies of Married Life
People and Other Aggravations
How Did I Get to Be Forty and Other Atrocities
If I Were in Charge of the World and Other Worries
Forever Fifty and Other Negotiations
Sad Underwear and Other Complications
Suddenly Sixty and Other Shocks of Later Life
I'm Too Young to Be Seventy and Other Delusions

CHILDREN' S BOOKS

Sunday Morning
I'll Fix Anthony
Try It Again, Sam
The Tenth Good Thing About Barney
Alexander and the Terrible, Horrible, No Good, Very Bad Day
My Mama Says There Aren't Any Zombies, Ghosts, Vampires,
   Creatures, Demons, Monsters, Fiends, Goblins, or Things
Rosie and Michael
Alexander, Who Used to Be Rich Last Sunday
The Good-bye Book
Earrings!
The Alphabet From Z to A (With Much Confusion on the Way)
Alexander, Who's Not (Do You Hear Me? I Mean It!) Going to Move
Absolutely Positively Alexander
Super-Completely and Totally the Messiest
Just in Case

OTHER

Yes, Married
A Visit From St. Nicholas (To a Liberated Household)
Love & Guilt & the Meaning of Life, Etc.
Necessary Losses
Murdering Mr. Monti
Imperfect Control
You're Officially a Grown-Up
Grown-Up Marriage
Alexander and the Wonderful, Marvelous, Excellent, Terrific Ninety Days

WHEN DID I STOP BEING 20

AND OTHER INJUSTICES

SELECTED POEMS FROM SINGLE TO MID-LIFE

BY JUDITH VIORST

DESIGNED AND ILLUSTRATED BY JOHN ALCORN

SIMON & SCHUSTER
New York   London   Toronto   Sydney

Simon & Schuster
1230 Avenue of the Americas
New York, NY 10020

This Simon & Schuster hardcover edition October 2007

SIMON & SCHUSTER and colophon are registered trademarks of Simon & Schuster, Inc.

For information about special discounts for bulk purchases, please contact Simon & Schuster
Special Sales at 1-800-456-6798 or business@simonandschuster.com

Designed by John Alcorn

Manufactured in the United States of America

10   9   8   7   6   5   4   3   2   1

The Library of Congress has cataloged the original hardcover edition as follows:
Viorst, Judith.
    When did I stop being twenty and other injustices.
    I. Title.
PS3572.I6W5   1987   811'.54   87-12778
ISBN 0-671-64328-2

ISBN-13: 978-1-4165-4866-9
ISBN-10:   1-4165-4866-1

Greatful acknowledgment is made for permission to reprint the following:
Poems from *How Did I Get to Be 40 and Other Atrocities* by Judith Viorst, copyright © 1973,
1974, 1976 by Judith Viorst. By permission of Simon & Schuster, Inc.
Poems from *People and Other Aggravations* by Judith Viorst, copyright © 1969, 1970,
1971, by Judith Viorst.
Poems from *It's Hard to Be Hip Over Thirty and Other Tragedies of Married Life* by Judith Viorst,
copyright © 1968 by Judith Viorst.
Poems from *The Village Square* by Judith Viorst, copyright © 1965, 1966 by Judith Viorst.

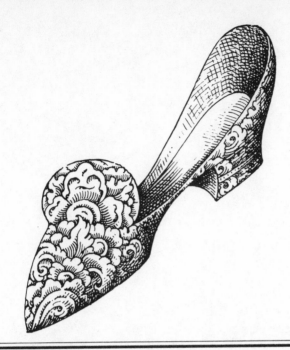

TO THE WOMEN
WHO HAVE
WALKED WITH ME
THROUGH
GREENWICH VILLAGE,
WASHINGTON
AND LIFE—

Hanna Altman
Sunny Aurelio
Jean Boudin
Ruth Caplin
Kitty Gillman
Liz Hersh
Phyllis Hersh
Ellie Horwitz
Silvia Koner
Leslie Oberdorfer
Sally Pitofsky
Shay Rieger
Barbara Rosenfeld
Lee Schorr
Judy Tolmach Silber

When Did I Stop Being Twenty
and Other Injustices

CONTENTS

VILLAGE LIFE

1 THE BREAK

2 THE APARTMENT

3 THE JOB

4 THE LOVERS

5 FOURTH STREET AND EIGHTH STREET

6 SEX IN THE VILLAGE

7 GREENWICH VILLAGE BABY

8 THE ORGY

9 HAPPINESS

10 I'LL NEVER TEACH MY PARENTS TO BE VILLAGE INTELLECTUALS

11 WILL I EVER GET MARRIED? (SONG OF THE SINGLE GIRL)

12 HENRY

CONTENTS

MARRIED LIFE

13 MARRIAGE AND THE FAMILIES

14 MARRIED IS BETTER

15 THE HONEYMOON IS OVER

16 MAYBE WE'LL MAKE IT

17 NICE BABY

18 MONEY

19 THE GOURMET

20 WHERE IS IT WRITTEN?

21 FAMILY REUNION

22 THE OTHER WOMAN

23 ANTI-HEROINE

24 A VISIT FROM MY MOTHER-IN-LAW

25 A WOMEN'S LIBERATION MOVEMENT WOMAN

26 THE SKI VACATION

27 STRIKING BACK

28 SEX IS NOT SO SEXY ANYMORE

29 INFIDELITY

30 TRUE LOVE

CONTENTS

MID~LIFE

31 THE TRUTH

32 NO MORE BABIES

33 COLLEGE REUNION

34 STARTING ON MONDAY

35 AMONG OTHER THOUGHTS ON OUR WEDDING ANNIVERSARY

36 MID-LIFE CRISIS

37 OPEN HOUSE

38 THREE IN THE MORNING

39 ALONE

40 SELF-IMPROVEMENT PROGRAM

41 FAMILIARITY BREEDS CONTENT (SONG OF THE LONG-MARRIED WOMAN)

42 ADULT EDUCATION

43 TWENTY QUESTIONS

44 FACING THE FACTS

VILLAGE LIFE

THE BREAK

So I told my parents:
No I do not believe in free love.
And yes I will be home for Sunday dinners.
And no I do not approve of marijuana.
And yes I will still take showers daily.
And no I will not turn out like my cousin Ethel.
(I think she is living with a married man in Tulsa.)
And yes I will get a police lock.
And eat a good breakfast every morning.
And only talk to men I am introduced to.

So they said:
If I must be independent
And make it hard for them to sleep nights,
I might as well do it in Greenwich Village,
Which at least isn't far from Irvington, New Jersey.

THE APARTMENT

Fifth-floor floor-through,
   no elevator.
Rear garden with fountain,
   no access.
Good-looking landlord,
   four children.

But:
The fireplace works.
Norman Mailer once attended a party on the second floor.
And Sheridan Square is just two blocks away.

Which is why I decided that:
It is not hard to wash dishes in a tub.
Roaches can be fun.
Falling plaster lends a certain charm.
And two hundred and ten dollars a month
Is a worthwhile investment for:
three beards
one dancer
one actress working as a waitress
one painter
one copywriter gathering material for a caustic denunciation of
   Madison Avenue
one dentist taking philosophy courses at the New School
   and
one insurance salesman
(maybe he'll move).

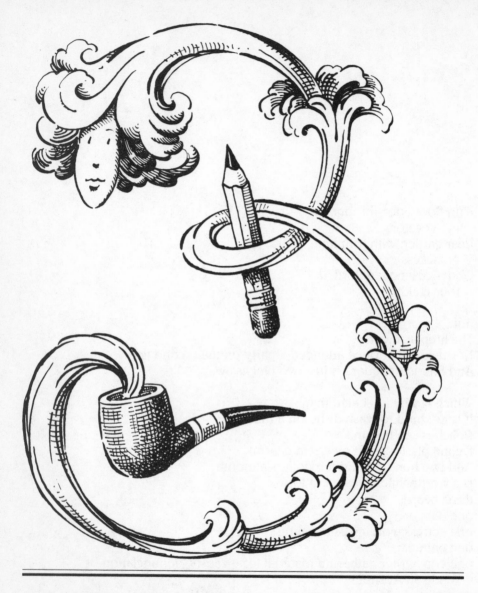

THE JOB

With all I know about Mr. D. H. Lawrence,
I visualized something literary,
Something full of pipe smoke and good English tweeds.
Where editors were stunned by my perception,
And grateful novelists put me in their books,
And Nobel prize winners, over double martinis,
Confided their deepest Nobel prize-winning thoughts
To tender, reflective, wise-beyond-my-years me.

With all I know about Mr. Stanislavsky,
I visualized something theatrical,
Something full of false lashes and empathy.
Where directors were stunned by my perception,
And grateful playwrights put me in their plays,
And leading ladies, over double martinis,
Said tearfully if only they had half the talent
Of stirring, memorable, charismatic me.

Instead of which
I am sharpening number two pencils,
And buying the coffee and Danish
At 9:45,
And taking my boss's dictation,
And my boss's wife's blouse back to Henri Bendel,
Hoping that someday someone will be impressed
With all I know.

THE LOVERS

In the Village
Boys can go with boys,
And girls with girls.

Different colored people
With different religions
Can go together.

Tall women can go
With short Master's Degrees
In Greek literature.

Suave old men
With two or three divorces
Can go with teenagers.

Curvy blondes
With empty heads
Can go with well-known thinkers.

There are no mothers around complaining
    that this isn't a good match.
There are no fathers walking back and forth saying
    is this why I sent you to Goucher.
There are no Aunt Eleanors calling up your parents
    to warn them before it's too late.

It is lovely to live in a place where
The only time folks think you're strange
Is if you go with an orthopedic surgeon.

FOURTH STREET AND EIGHTH STREET

Everything I need
Is on Fourth Street and Eighth Street:
    thong sandals and butterfly chairs
    mobiles
    doors that can be used as beds or couches or tables
    straw baskets that can be used for laundry or flowers.

Last week I went out shopping
On Fourth Street and Eighth Street.
    I bought a plaid poncho.
    I bought an African mask.
    I bought a few basics like a bottle of Chianti, a Japanese globe, and the
        Bach cantatas.
    I put a deposit on a dress you climb into from the neck and matching
        earrings.

There are still many things I have to buy,
All of which can be purchased on Fourth Street and Eighth Street:
    a brandy snifter
    a Van Gogh reproduction
    leotards
        and
    three doors.

It is very nice to know
That I don't need Lord & Taylor anymore.

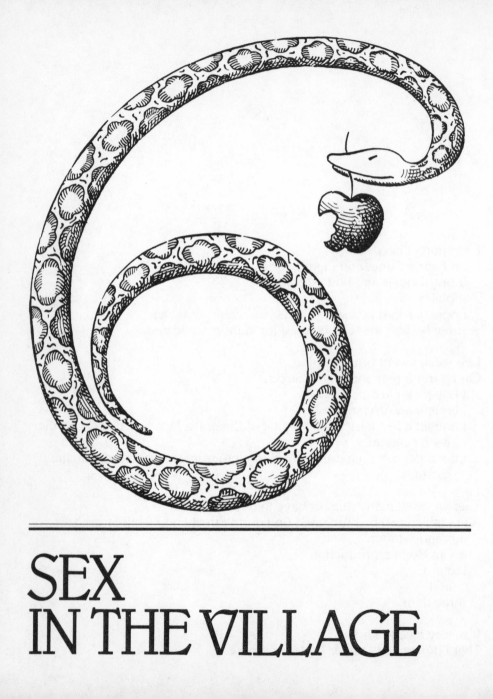

SEX
IN THE VILLAGE

Sex in the Village
Is much more complicated
Than it was in Irvington, New Jersey.
In Irvington, New Jersey, a girl could look shocked,
Even if she wasn't,
And explain that she wanted to remain a virgin,
Even if she didn't.

At least nobody laughed.

In Irvington, New Jersey, I was considered very smooth.
But after three months in the Village I have been called:
    emotionally immature
    bourgeois
    masochistic
    prejudiced against NYU law students
    unfeminine
    unrealistic
        and
    undersexed.

I am trying to work out a new attitude,
But it will take time.
Sex in the Village is very complicated.

GREENWICH
VILLAGE BABY

Irvington children are usually Peters and Debbies
Who eat Cap'n Crunch in vinyl dining areas,
Go to Radio City Music Hall in car pools,
And brush after every meal.

That is not the kind of child I have in mind.

Someday I'll have a Greenwich Village baby,
The kind who likes Vivaldi when he's three.
Has too much hair, no shoes, a high IQ,
And his own analyst.

I'll feed my baby Camembert and paté.
He'll only watch the finest N.E.T.,
While his father—the poet—sits in a sling chair
Writing a sonnet.

I will not raise my son to be a doctor.
He will not have to love his dad or me.
I'll be content with any girl he chooses,
As long as she pickets.

Someday I'll have a Greenwich Village baby,
At seventeen he'll have his Ph.D.
At twenty-five his Andrea and Luke
Will play in the sandbox at Washington Square
While their grandmother—the medieval scholar—
Sits on a bench
Reading Aquinas in Latin.

THE ORGY

I wanted to go to the orgy.

I'd been thinking about it for weeks.
It was just going to be a little orgy
With a few friends.

I was ready to abandon myself
To my most primitive emotions
Or whatever it is that you do
At orgies.

I really wanted to go.
But Friday night came around and there I was
With the sniffles.
And a stomach ache.
And I think I twisted my ankle getting off the bus.
And my stockings hadn't dried.
And I couldn't find a clean slip.
And my mother called to ask me what was new.

So I wound up staying home
Washing underwear and taking aspirin
Instead of going to the orgy.

And I really wanted to go.

HAPPINESS

Happiness
Is eating prunewhip yogurt
On the floor
And discussing the meaning of it all
With very profound people
Who have so much integrity
That they cannot afford shoemakers or taxis.

Happiness
Is my mother calling at four in the morning
But I'm still not home.
And walking barefoot down Grove Street
With very profound people
Who can name all the brothers Karamazov
But are too cool to do so.

And someday,
When a Greek shipping magnate offers,
In return for my love,
Matched black pearls,
And minks and sables galore,
Along with a Jaguar,
A custom-built yacht,
And a house in Martha's Vineyard
To alternate with the Fifth Avenue co-operative,
I will tell him
What happiness
Is.

I'LL NEVER TEACH MY PARENTS TO BE VILLAGE INTELLECTUALS

Last Sunday,
After the chicken and noodles in Irvington,
I asked my mother point-blank
Whether she would rather be a pig satisfied
Or Socrates unsatisfied.
She said, "Don't you call me a pig."

And then I asked my father
Whether he thought the sexually inhibited middle class
Would ever cast off its hypocritical restraints
And acknowledge the pleasures of orgiastic excess.
He put down the sports page and told me,
"Don't talk dirty."

I'll never teach my parents to be Village intellectuals.
They just don't want to benefit from all the things I know.
I come each week with reading lists to elevate their view of life.
I think they always watch TV the minute that I go.

I bring them Portuguese on tape to study while they sleep at night.
I tell them if they concentrate there's still a chance to grow.
I bring them nice Picasso prints to hang up in the breakfast nook.
I think they always take them down the minute that I go.

I'll never teach my parents to be Village intellectuals.
They like gin rummy better than they like Jean-Jacques Rousseau.
They listen quite politely while I clarify world thought for them.
I think they always laugh at me the minute that I go.

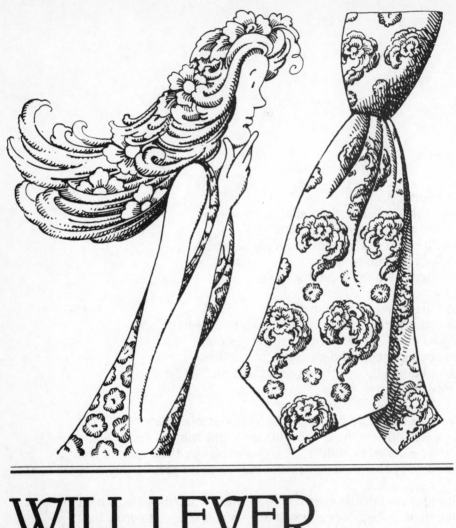

WILL I EVER GET MARRIED?
(SONG OF THE SINGLE GIRL)

Will I ever get married?
Is the end of my searching in sight?
There are lamps that I'm waiting to light,
Waiting to light them together.

Will I ever get married?
There are secrets my heart yearns to speak
To that someone who seeks what I seek,
And wants to seek it together.

The world is full of short-term lovers
Who don't even know your middle name.
I want to snuggle under the covers
Year after year after year after year
With the same . . .

With the same man.

Will I ever get married?
Will I ever be somebody's wife?
Making dinner, love, babies, a life,
Making a life together.

HENRY

I have fallen in love.
His name is Henry and he is against all my principles.

He is not an older man.
He does not have a beard.
He likes his family.
He eats his steak well done.

He thinks the country is better than the city.
He thinks ice hockey is better than poetry readings.
He doesn't believe one must fight to the death against all bourgeois
    values.
He doesn't even smoke.

But I have fallen in love.
And so has he.

Henry says I'm a nice girl even though I live in the Village.
He says I will make a fine mother.
He says I will adore skiing.

This was not the image I intended to project.

But I have fallen in love.
And I will have to choose between Sheridan Square and Henry.
Between paella à la Valenciana and Henry.
Between buying books and records and a quarter's worth of daffodils at
    two in the morning and Henry.

I never dreamed I'd end up marrying a man
My parents would approve of.

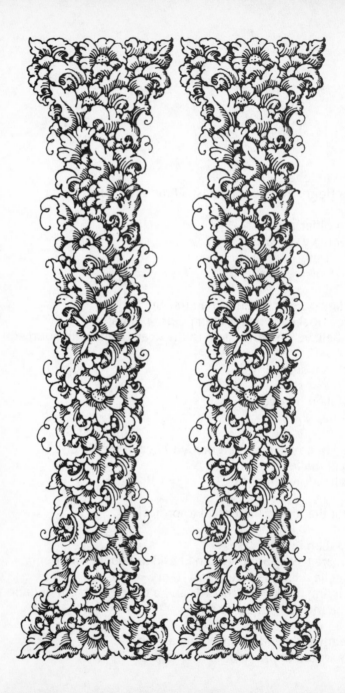

MARRIED LIFE

MARRIAGE AND THE FAMILIES

My mother was grateful
He wasn't barefoot.
His mother was grateful
I wasn't pregnant.

My father was grateful
He wasn't of a different race, color, or creed.
His father was grateful
I wasn't tubercular or divorced.

My sister was grateful
Her husband was richer and taller.
His sister was grateful
She had a master's degree and a better nose.

My cousin in luggage was grateful
He didn't expect a discount.
His cousin the dentist was grateful
I didn't need root canal.

My aunts and my uncles were grateful
He came from a nice family in New Jersey even though he wore
    sunglasses in the living room which is usually a sign of depravity.
His aunts and his uncles were grateful
I came from a nice family in New Jersey even though I lived in
    Greenwich Village which is usually a sign of depravity also.

I should be pleased.

But when I think of the catered wedding in Upper Montclair,
With the roast sirloin of beef dinner,
The souvenir photo album,
And the matches with our names in raised gold letters,
And when I think of the savings bonds, the china, the cut glass,
    and the sugars and creamers both sterling and silver plate,
Then I wish
That they weren't
So grateful.

MARRIED IS BETTER

Married is better
Than sitting on a blanket in Nantucket
Where you get blotches and a red nose instead of adorable
    freckles and golden brown.
Hoping that someone with whom you would not be caught dead
From September to June
Will invite you to dinner.

And married is better
Than riding a double chair lift up at Stowe
On your way to an expert trail and you're a beginner,
Hoping the fellow for whom you are risking your life
Will invite you to dinner.
And one night, when you land at Kennedy,
And no one is there to meet you except your parents,
And you suddenly realize that you never saw the Parthenon
Because you were too busy looking around for a Greek god,
You also suddenly realize
Married is better.

And married is better
Than an affair with a marvelous man
Who would leave his wife immediately except that she would slash
    her wrists and the children would cry.
So instead you drink his Scotch in your living room and never
    meet his friends because they might become disillusioned or
    tell,
And when it's your birthday it's his evening with the in-laws,
And when it's his birthday he can't even bring home your present
(Because of the slashed wrists and the crying and all),
So even though you have his body and soul while his wife only
    has his laundry and the same name,
You somehow begin to suspect
Married is better.

And married is better
Than the subway plus a crosstown bus every morning,
And tuna on toasted cheese bread, no lettuce, at Schrafft's.
And a bachelor-girl apartment with burlap and foam rubber and a
    few droll touches like a samurai sword in the bathroom,
And going to the movies alone,
And worrying that one morning you'll wake up and discover you're
    an older woman,
And always projecting wholesome sexuality combined with
    independence, femininity, and tons of outside interests,
And never for a minute letting on
That deep in your heart you believe
Married is better.

THE
HONEYMOON
IS OVER

The honeymoon is over
And he has left for work
Whistling something obvious from La Bohème
And carrying a brown calfskin attaché case
I never dreamed he was capable of owning.
Having started the day
With ten push-ups and a cold shower
Followed by a hearty breakfast.

(What do we actually have in common?)

The honeymoon is over
And I am dry-mopping the floor
In a green Dacron dry-mopping outfit from Saks,
Wondering why I'm not dancing in the dark,
Or rejecting princes,
Or hearing people gasp at my one-man show,
My god, so beautiful and so gifted!

(The trouble is, I never knew a prince.)

The honeymoon is over
And we find that dining by candlelight makes us squint,
And that all the time
I was letting him borrow my comb and hang up his wet raincoat
   in my closet,
I was really waiting
To stop letting him.
And that all the time
He was saying how he loved my chicken pot pie,
He was really waiting
To stop eating it.

(I guess they call this getting to know each other.)

MAYBE
WE'LL MAKE IT

If I quit hoping he'll show up with flowers, and
He quits hoping I'll squeeze him an orange, and
I quit shaving my legs with his razor, and
He quits wiping his feet with my face towel, and
We avoid discussions like
Is he really smarter than I am, or simply more glib,
Maybe we'll make it.

If I quit looking to prove that he's hostile, and
He quits looking for dust on the tables, and
I quit inviting Louise with the giggle, and
He quits inviting Jerome with the complex, and
We avoid discussions like
Suppose I died, which one of our friends would he marry,
Maybe we'll make it.

If I quit clearing the plates while he's eating, and
He quits clearing his throat while I'm speaking, and
I quit implying I could have done better, and
He quits implying he wishes I had, and
We avoid discussions like
Does his mother really love him, or is she simply one of those
     over-possessive, devouring women who can't let go,
Maybe we'll make it.

NICE BABY

Last year I talked about black humor and the impact of the common
    market on the European economy and
Threw clever little cocktail parties in our discerningly eclectic
    living room
With the Spanish rug and the hand-carved Chinese chest and the
    lucite chairs and
Was occasionally hungered after by highly placed men in
    communications, but
This year we have a nice baby
And Pablum drying on our Spanish rug,
And I talk about nursing versus sterilization
While the men in communications
Hunger elsewhere.

Last year I studied flamenco and had my ears pierced and
Served an authentic fondue on the Belgian marble table of our
    discerningly eclectic dining area, but
This year we have a nice baby
And Spock on the second shelf of our Chinese chest,
And instead of finding myself I am doing my best
To find a sitter
For the nice baby banging the Belgian marble with his cup
While I heat the oven up
For the TV dinners.

Last year I had a shampoo and set every week and
Slept an unbroken sleep beneath the Venetian chandelier of our
    discerningly eclectic bedroom, but
This year we have a nice baby,
And Gerber's strained bananas in my hair,
And gleaming beneath the Venetian chandelier,
A diaper pail, a Portacrib, and him,
A nice baby, drooling on our antique satin spread
While I smile and say how nice. It is often said
That motherhood is very maturing.

MONEY

Once I aspired to
Humble black turtleneck sweaters
And spare unheated rooms
With the Kama Sutra, a few madrigals, and
Great literature and philosophy.

Once I considered money
Something to be against
On the grounds that
Credit cards,
Installment-plan buying,
And a joint checking account
Could never coexist with
Great literature and philosophy.

Once I believed
That the only kind of marriage I could respect
Was a spiritual relationship
Between two wonderfully spiritual human beings
Who would never argue about money
Because they would be too busy arguing about
Great literature and philosophy.

I changed my mind
Having discovered that

Spiritual is hard without the cash
To pay the plumber to unstop the sink
And pay a lady to come clean and iron
So every other Friday I can think about
Great literature and philosophy.

No one ever offers us a choice
Between the Kama Sutra and a yacht.
We're always selling out for diaper service
And other drab necessities that got ignored in
Great literature and philosophy.

A jug of wine, a loaf of bread, and thou
No longer will suffice. I must confess
My consciousness is frequently expanded
By MasterCard, American Express, and things undreamed of in
Great literature and philosophy.

I saw us walking hand-in-hand through life,
But now it's clear we really need two cars.
I looked with such contempt at power mowers,
But now, alas, that power mower's ours.
It seems I'm always reaching for my charge plates,
When all I'd planned to reach for were the stars,
Great literature and philosophy.

THE GOURMET

My husband grew up eating lox in New Jersey,
But now he eats saumon fumé.
The noshes he once used to nosh before dinner
He's calling hors d'oeuvres variés.
And food is cuisine since he learned how to be a gourmet.

He now has a palate instead of a stomach
And must have his salad après,
His ris de veau firm, and his Port Salut runny,
All ordered, of course, en français,
So the waiter should know he is serving a full-fledged gourmet.

No meal is complete without something en croute, a-
Mandine, béchamel, en gelée,
And those wines he selects with the care that a surgeon
Transplanting a heart might display.
He keeps sniffing the corks since he learned how to be a gourmet.

The tans some folks get from a trip to St. Thomas
He gets from the cerises flambées,
After which he requires, instead of a seltzer,
A cognac or Grand Marnier,
With a toast to the chef from my husband the nouveau gourmet.

The words people use for a Chartres or a Mozart
He's using to praise a soufflé.
He reads me aloud from James Beard and Craig Claiborne
The way others read from Corneille.
And he's moved by a mousse since he learned how to be a gourmet.

But back in New Jersey, whenever we visit,
They don't know from Pouilly-Fuissé.
They're still serving milk in the glass from the jelly.
They still cook the brisket all day.
And a son who can't finish three helpings is not a gourmet.

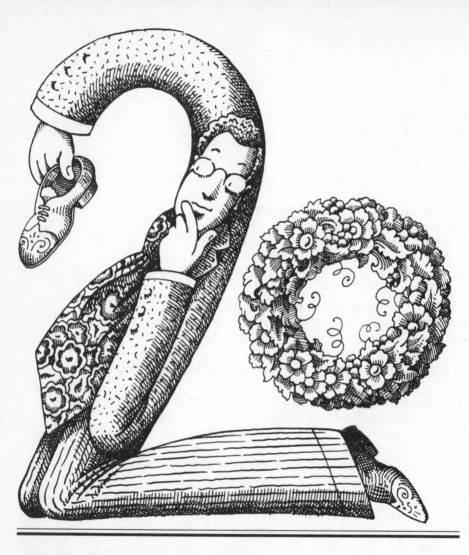

WHERE IS IT WRITTEN?

Where is it written
That husbands get forty-five-dollar lunches and invitations to
    South America for think conferences while
Wives get Campbell's black bean soup and a trip to the firehouse
    with the third grade and
Where is it written
That husbands get to meet beautiful lady lawyers and beautiful
    lady professors of ancient history and beautiful sculptresses
    and heiresses and poetesses while
Wives get to meet the checker with the acne at the Safeway and
Where is it written
That husbands get a nap and the football game on Sundays while
Wives get to help color in the coloring book and
Where is it written
That husbands get ego gratification, emotional support, and hot
    tea in bed for ten days when they have the sniffles while
Wives get to give it to them?

And if a wife should finally decide
Let him take the shoes to the shoemaker and the children to the
    pediatrician and the dog to the vet while she takes up
    something like brain surgery or transcendental meditation,
Where is it written
That she always has to feel
Guilty?

FAMILY REUNION

The first full-fledged family reunion
Was held at the seashore
With twelve pounds of sturgeon
Nine pounds of corned beef
One nephew who got the highest mark on an intelligence test
    ever recorded in Hillside, New Jersey
Four aunts in pain taking pills
One cousin in analysis taking notes
One sister-in-law who makes a cherry cheese cake a person
    would be happy to pay to eat
Five uncles to whom what happened in the stock market shouldn't
    happen to their worst enemy
One niece who is running away from home the minute the
    orthodontist removes her braces
One cousin you wouldn't believe it to look at him only likes
    fellows
One nephew involved with a person of a different racial
    persuasion which his parents are taking very well
One brother-in-law with a house so big you could get lost and
    carpeting so thick you could suffocate and a mortgage so high
    you could go bankrupt
One uncle whose wife is a saint to put up with him
One cousin who has made such a name for himself he was almost
    Barbra Streisand's gynecologist
One cousin who has made such a name for himself he was almost
    Elizabeth Taylor's CPA
One cousin don't ask what he does for a living
One niece it wouldn't surprise anyone if next year she's playing
    at Carnegie Hall
One nephew it wouldn't surprise anyone if next year he's
    sentenced to Leavenworth
Two aunts who used to go to the same butcher as Philip Roth's
    mother
And me wanting approval from all of them.

THE OTHER
WOMAN

The other woman
Never smells of Ajax or Spaghetti-O,
And was bored with Bob Dylan
A year before we had heard of him,
And is a good sport about things like flat tires and no hot
    water,
Because it's easier to be a good sport
When you're not married.

The other woman
Never has tired blood,
And can name the best hotels in Acapulco
As readily as we can name detergents,
And wears a chiffon peignoir instead of a corduroy bathrobe,
Because it's easier to try harder
When you're not married.

The other woman
Never has to look at Secret Squirrel,
And spends her money on fun furs
While we are spending ours on obstetricians,
And can make a husband feel that he is wanted,
Because it's easier to want a husband
When you're not married.

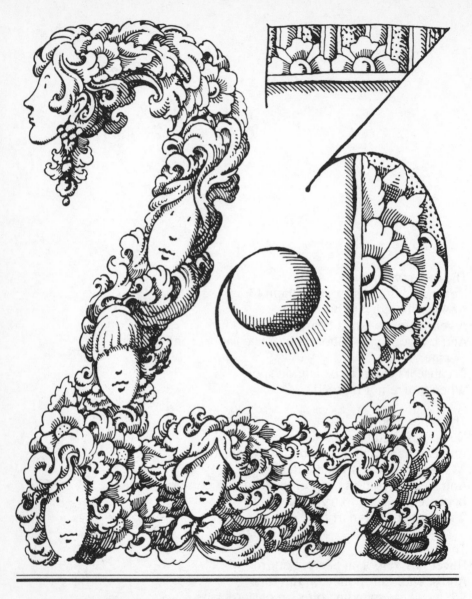

ANTI-HEROINE

I'd planned to be Heathcliff's Cathy, Lady Brett,
Nicole or Dominique or Scarlett O'Hara.
I hadn't planned to be folding up the laundry
In uncombed hair and last night's smudged mascara,
An expert on buying Fritos, cleaning the cat box,
Finding lost sneakers, playing hide-and-seek,
And other things unknown to Heathcliff's Cathy,
Scarlett, Lady Brett, and Dominique.

Why am I never running through the heather?
Why am I never raped by Howard Roark?
Why am I never going to Pamplona
Instead of Philadelphia and Newark?
How did I ever wind up with a Henry,
When what I'd always had in mind was Rhett,
Or someone more appropriate to Cathy,
Dominique, Nicole, or Lady Brett.

I saw myself as heedless, heartless, headstrong,
An untamed woman searching for her mate.
And there he is—with charcoal, fork, and apron,
Prepared to broil some hot dogs on the grate.
I haven't wrecked his life or his digestion
With unrequited love or jealous wrath. He
Doesn't know that secretly I'm Scarlett,
Dominique, Nicole, or Brett, or Cathy.

Why am I never cracking up in Zurich?
Why am I never languishing on moors?
Why am I never spoiled by faithful mammys
Instead of spraying ant spray on the floors?
The tricycles are cluttering my foyer.
The Pop-Tart crumbs are sprinkled on my soul.
And every year it's harder to be Cathy,
Dominique, Brett, Scarlett, and Nicole.

A VISIT
FROM MY
MOTHER-IN-LAW

My mother-in-law
Comes to visit
With her own apron,
Her own jar of Nescafe,
And the latest news.

Uncle Leo,
She's sorry to say,
Is divorcing Aunt Pearl,
Whose sister Bernice
Is having
A nervous breakdown.
The week
That they spent in Miami
It rained every day,
And her health,
Though she isn't complaining,
Has never been worse.
The lady upstairs
With the limp
Was attacked in broad daylight,
And Seymour her nephew
Has cataracts, flu,
And no job.
My husband,
She thinks she should mention,
Looks thin as a rail,
And the children,
It hurts her to hear,
Are coughing again.
Belle's son,
Only forty years old,
Dropped dead Friday morning,
And don't even bother
To ask
About Cousin Rose.

I don't think I will.

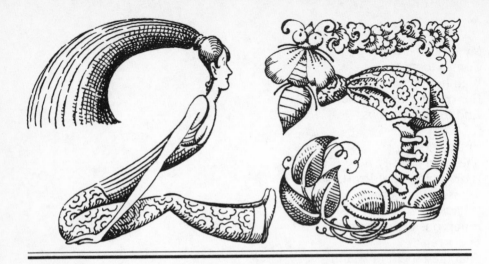

A WOMEN'S LIBERATION MOVEMENT WOMAN

When it's snowing and I put on all the galoshes
While he reads the paper,
Then I want to become a
Women's Liberation Movement woman.
And when it's snowing and he looks for the taxi
While I wait in the lobby,
Then I don't.

And when it's vacation and I'm in charge of mosquito bites
    and poison ivy and car sickness
While he's in charge of swimming,
Then I want to become a
Women's Liberation Movement woman.
And when it's vacation and he carries the suitcases
    and the bicycles and the playpen
While I carry the tote bag,
Then I don't.

And when it's three in the morning and the baby definitely needs
    a glass of water and I have to get up and bring it
While he keeps my place warm,
Then I want to become a
Women's Liberation Movement woman.
And when it's three in the morning and there is definitely a
    murderer-rapist in the vestibule and he has to get up and catch him
While I keep his place warm,
Then I don't.

And after dinner, when he talks to the company
While I clean the broiler
(because I am a victim of capitalism, imperialism, male
    chauvinism, and also Playboy magazine),
And afternoons, when he invents the telephone and wins the
    Dreyfus case and writes War and Peace
While I sort the socks
(because I am economically oppressed, physically exploited,
    psychologically mutilated, and also very insulted),
And after he tells me that it is genetically determined that the
    man makes martinis and the lady makes the beds
(because he sees me as a sex object, an earth mother, a domestic
    servant, and also dumber than he is),
Then I want to become a
Women's Liberation Movement woman.

And after I consider
Having justice,
Having equality,
Having freedom,
And also having
To change my own tires,
Then I want it
Both ways.

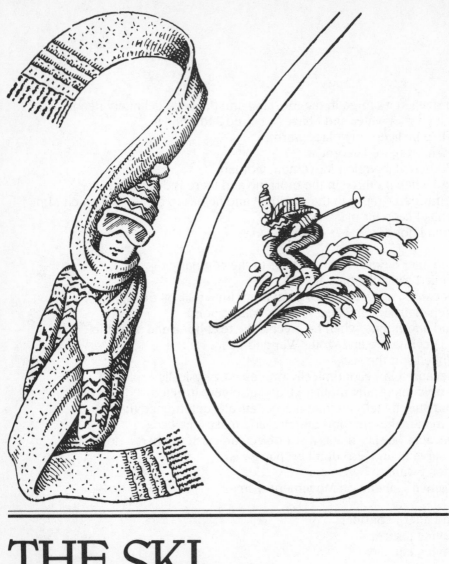

THE SKI
VACATION

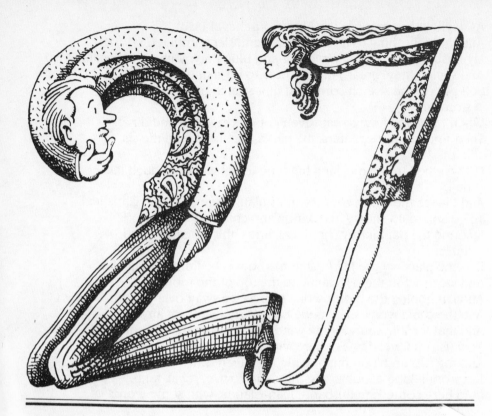

STRIKING BACK

When a husband tells a wife
Stop screaming at the children
And he isn't crazy about the drapes
And why doesn't she learn where Thailand is
And maybe she should cut her hair
(All of which, needless to say, are implicit attacks on her
    intelligence, taste, desirability, and maternal instincts)
A wife
Can only
Strike back.

As daylight breaks over the Alps (Courchevel 1850),
And the right thing to do is roll over and sleep until ten,
My husband is nudging my black-and-blue thigh with his kneecap,
And saying (hey, great!) that it's time to go skiing again.
So I put on the stretch pants that quit stretching over my
    stomach
When I learned how to eat seven courses at lunch and dîner,
Then I put on the sweaters, the parka, the hood, and the ski
    boots
(They're hell in the morning but tend to get worse through the
    day),
And I leave the warm room with its blankets and Agatha Christies
To go where it's snowy and windy and cold and not safe,
Ignoring the pain in my shoulders, arms, thighs, calves, and
    ankles,
Plus the place where the heel in my boot is beginning to chafe.
And we're off in the télécabine to the top of the mountain
And I'm hoping the motor won't stop as we sway over peaks,
And the cable won't snap as we hang forty feet from abysses,
And that terrible sound is the wind and not somebody's shrieks.
Now (isn't it lovely!) we're here with the treetops below us,
And my skis aren't on but already I've fallen down twice
Just from taking a look at the trail—narrow, vertical, fatal.
(And here comes my husband, Jean-Claude, with some words of
    advice.)
Well, I've just cut my thumb in the process of closing my
    bindings,
And my goggles are fogged and my nerves inexpressibly shot.
But I'm off with a wild snowplow turn and a large crowd of
    Frenchmen,
Who keep schussing past me with shouts of à gauche and à droite.
And I know I could tell which was which if I wasn't attempting
To bend at the knees, shift my weight, not go over that ledge,
Which explains why I've skied off the trail and am presently
    standing
In uncharted mountains and up to my fesses in the neige,
Where I'm dreaming of tropical isles, riding surf in bikinis,
But willing to settle for home, pushing kids in the carriage,
And firmly convinced that the Alps may be swell for the Killys,
But not for a person who's only a skier by marriage.

So sometimes I try
My mother's technique
Which is silence for a week,
A brooding stare into the ruined future,
And no rouge for that look of
You are making me so miserable you are giving me
A fatal illness.

It occasionally works.

And sometimes I try
Weeping, cursing, expressions of bitter remorse,
And don't ever expect to see the children again,
Which I often follow with phone calls pricing suites
At expensive hotels.

I've had limited success.

There is also the psychoanalytic confrontation
Which entails informing him
(More, of course, in sorrow than in anger)
That his sadistic treatment of those who love him is a sign of
    unconscious feelings of inadequacy and
He needs help.

I've dropped this approach.

But there is always
Total recall
During which all the wrongs he has done me since first we met
    are laid before him.
And when this is combined
With refusing to go to the Greenbergs' annual costume party,
Tossing and moaning in my sleep,
And threatening to commit suicide, take a lover, and drop out of
    the PTA because why try to save the school system when my
    entire universe is falling apart,
I start to feel
I'm really
Striking back.

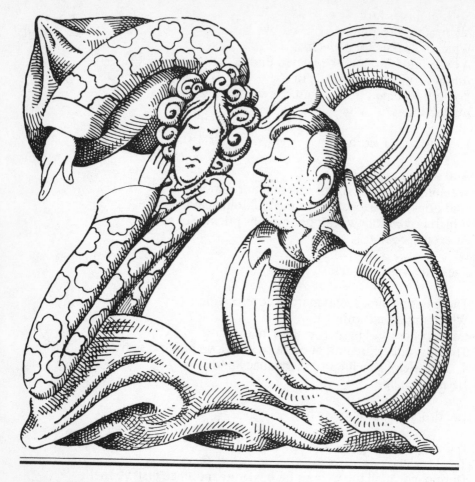

SEX IS NOT SO SEXY ANYMORE

I bring the children one more glass of water.
I rub the hormone night cream on my face.
Then after I complete the isometrics,
I greet my husband with a warm embrace,

A vision in my long-sleeved flannel nightgown
And socks (because my feet are always freezing),
Gulping tranquilizers for my nerve ends
And Triaminic tablets for my wheezing.

Our blue electric blanket's set for toasty.
Our red alarm clock's set at seven-thirty.
I tell him that we owe the grocer plenty.
He tells me that his two best suits are dirty.

Last year I bought him Centaur for his birthday.
(They promised he'd become half-man, half-beast.)
Last year he bought me something black and lacy.
(They promised I'd go mad with lust, at least.)

Instead my rollers clink upon the pillow
And his big toenail scrapes against my shin.
He rises to apply a little Chap Stick.
I ask him to bring back two Bufferin.

Oh somewhere there are lovely little boudoirs
With Porthault sheets and canopies and whips.
He lion-hunts in Africa on weekends.
She measures thirty-three around the hips.

Their eyes engage across the brandy snifters.
He runs his fingers through her Kenneth hair.
The kids are in the other wing with nanny.
The sound of violins is everywhere.

In our house there's the sound of dripping water.
It's raining and he never patched the leak.
He grabs the mop and I get out the bucket.
We both agree to try again next week.

INFIDELITY

In my burnt-orange Dynel lounging pajamas
With the rhinestone buttons,
I was, I concede, looking more abandoned than usual,
Which is probably why
My husband's best friend
Made overtures.

My pulse quickened
And I could imagine . . .
    Cryptic conversations.
    Clandestine martinis.
    Tumultuous embraces.
    And me explaining
    That I can't slip away on Thursdays because of Cub Scouts,
    And that long kisses clog my sinuses.

Under the bridge table
His hand-sewn moccasins
Rubbed insistently against my Bernardo sandals
While Dionne Warwick
Sang something suggestive
In stereo.

My lips trembled,
And I could imagine . . .
    Stolen weekends at a windswept beach.
    Waves pounding on the shore.
    And pounding on the door
    Of our motel hideaway,
    The Vice Squad.

Over the salt-free peanuts and diet soda
His contact lenses
Sought mine,
As I sucked in my stomach
And asked him,
Coffee or Sanka?

My throat tightened,
My lips trembled,
My pulse quickened . . .
    But aggravation
    Was all
    I could imagine.

TRUE LOVE

It's true love because
I put on eyeliner and a concerto and make pungent observations
    about the great issues of the day
Even when there's no one here but him.
And because
I do not resent watching the Green Bay Packers
Even though I am philosophically opposed to football.
And because
When he is late for dinner and I know he must be either having
    an affair or lying dead in the middle of the street,
I always hope he's dead.

It's true love because
If he said quit drinking martinis but I kept drinking them and
    the next morning I couldn't get out of bed,
He wouldn't tell me he told me,
And because
He is willing to wear unironed undershorts
Out of respect for the fact that I am philosophically opposed
    to ironing.
And because
If his mother was drowning and I was drowning and he had to
    choose one of us to save,
He says he'd save me.

It's true love because
When he went to San Francisco on business while I had to stay
    home with the painters and the exterminator and the baby
    who was getting chicken pox,
He understood why I hated him,
And because
When I said that playing the stock market was juvenile and
    irresponsible and then the stock I wouldn't let him buy
    went up twenty-six points,
I understood why he hated me,
And because
Despite cigarette cough, tooth decay, acid indigestion, dandruff,
    and other features of married life that tend to dampen the
    fires of passion,
We still feel something
We can call
True love.

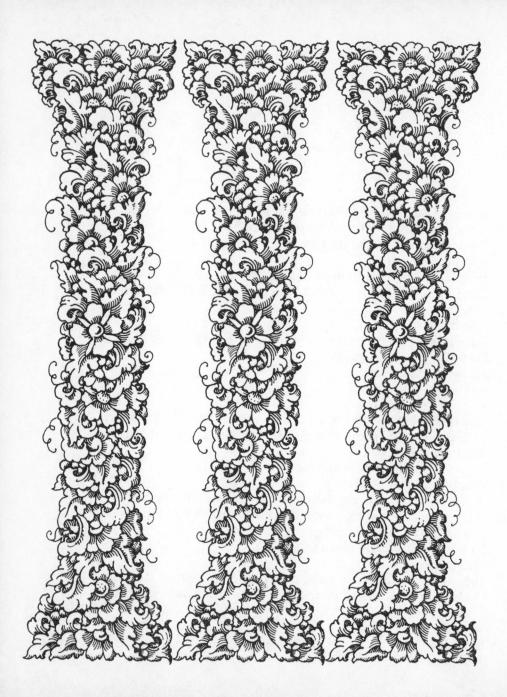

MID~LIFE

THE TRUTH

The truth is
If I had it all to do over
I still wouldn't study Swahili,
Learn to fly a plane,
Or take 92 lovers,
Some of them simultaneously.

The truth is
If I lived my life again
I still wouldn't leap before looking,
I still wouldn't count my chickens before they were hatched,
And I'd still, just in case I was hit by a car and had to be
    rushed to the hospital and examined,
Wear clean underwear.

The truth is
If I got a second chance
I still wouldn't know a forward pass from a backward one,
A self-effacing wine from a presumptuous one,
Or a man who, if I let him pick me up, would be rich, sincere,
    and of the same religious persuasion
From a man who, if I let him pick me up, would wind up being a
    homicidal rapist.

The truth is
That I'll always want to be
Pure enough to hate white bread,
Deep enough to admire Patagonian folk art,
Thin enough to go swimming in the nude,
Mature enough to outgrow Erich Fromm,
Nice enough to be nice to my Uncle Bernie,
And secure enough to not need getting married.

But the truth is
That the next time around,
I still wouldn't.

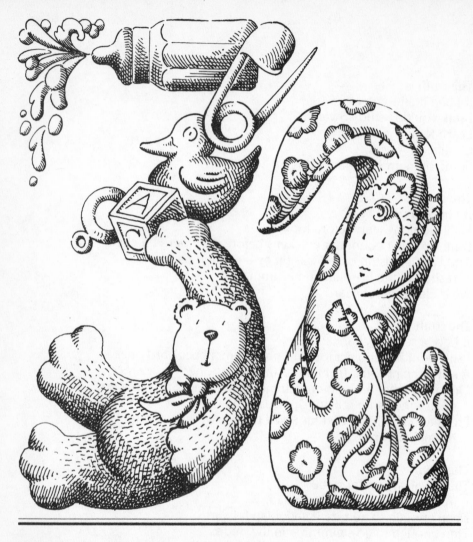

NO MORE
BABIES

The sterilizer's up for grabs.
Nicked Portacrib, goodbye.
My third and youngest son is growing older.
I'm done with dawn awakenings,
With Pablum in my eye,
With small moist bundles burping on my shoulder.

I gave away my drawstring slacks
And smocks with floppy bows.
My silhouette will never more be pear-ish.
And though I'm left with stretch marks
And a few veins varicose,
I'm aiming for an image less ma-mère-ish.

No playpens in the living room
Will mangle my décor.
My stairs will not be blocked with safety fences.
No rattles, bottles, bibs, stuffed bears
Will disarray my floor,
No eau de diaper pail assail my senses.

And no more babies will disrupt
The tenor of my days,
Nor croup and teething interrupt my sleeping.
I swear to you I wouldn't have it
Any other way.
It's positively stupid to be weeping.

COLLEGE
REUNION

We've all turned into women with a matching set of luggage
      and a butcher for our special cuts of meat,
And trouble getting to sleep if our room is too stuffy, too cold,
      or not quiet enough, or the pillow is hard, or our sheet isn't
Tightly tucked in at the bottom.

And we've all turned into women with a standing hair appointment
      and an air-conditioned car and name-brand bag,
And some drop-out Buddhist vegetarian Maoist children to
Aggravate us.

And we've all turned into women who know genuine in jewelry and
      authentic in antiques and real in fur,
And the best in orthopedists for our frequently recurring
Lower back pain.

And we've all turned into women who take cars instead of buses
      and watch color, not the black-and-white, TV,
And have lawyers, gynecologists, accountants, dermatologists,
      podiatrists, urologists, internists, cardiologists,
      insurance agents, travel agents, brokers, ophthalmologists,
And no idea how we all turned into these women.

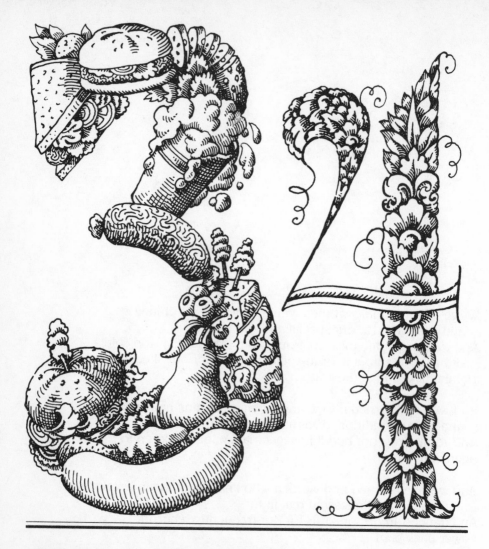

STARTING
ON MONDAY

Starting on Monday I'm living on carrots and bouillon.
Starting on Monday I'm bidding the bagel adieu.
I'm switching from Hersheys with almonds to gaunt and anemic.
And people will ask me could that skinny person be you.
I'll count every calorie from squash (half a cup, 47)
To Life Saver (8), stalk of celery (5), pepper ring (2),
Starting on Monday.

Starting on Monday I'll jog for a mile in the morning.
(That's after the sit-ups and push-ups and touching my toes.)
The gratification I once used to seek in lasagna
I'll find on the day that I have to go buy smaller clothes.
I'll turn my attention from infantile pleasures like Clark Bars
To things like the song of a bird and the scent of a rose,
Starting on Monday.

Starting on Monday my will will be stronger than brownies,
And anything more than an unsalted egg will seem crude.
My inner-thigh fat and my upper-arm flab will diminish.
My cheeks will be hollowed, my ribs will begin to protrude.
The bones of my pelvis will make their initial appearance—
A testament to my relentless abstention from food,
Starting on Monday.

But Tuesday a friend came for coffee and brought homemade muffins.
And Wednesday I had to quit jogging because of my back.
On Thursday I read in the paper an excess of egg yolk
Would clog up my vessels and certainly cause an attack.
On Friday we ate at the Altmans'. She always makes cream sauce,
And always gets sulky if people don't eat what she makes.
On Saturday evening we went with the kids to a drive-in.
I begged for a Fresca but all they were selling were shakes.
On Sunday my stomach oozed over the top of my waistband,
And filled with self-loathing I sought consolation in pie
And the thought that a millionaire could bribe me with diamonds
But still I'd refuse to taste even a single French fry,
Starting on Monday.

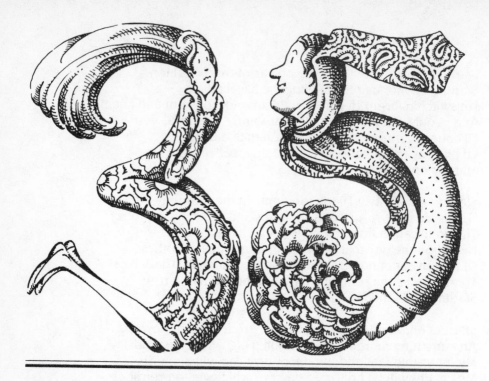

AMONG OTHER THOUGHTS ON OUR WEDDING ANNIVERSARY

Over the years,
When the sink overflowed
Or the car ran out of gas
Or the lady who comes every Friday to clean didn't come
Or I felt pudgy
Or misunderstood
Or inferior to Marilyn Kaufman who is not only a pediatric
    surgeon but also a very fine person as well as beautiful
Or I fell in the creek and got soaked on our first family
    camping trip
Or I bruised my entire left side on our first family camping
    trip
Or I walked through a patch of what later turned out to be plenty
    of poison ivy on what later turned out to be our last family
    camping trip
Or my sweater shrank in the wash
Or I stepped on my glasses
Or the keys that I swear on my children's heads I put on the top
    of the dresser weren't there
Or I felt depressed
Or unfulfilled
Or inferior to Ellen Jane Garver who not only teaches constitu-
    tional law but is also a wit plus sexually insatiable
Or they lost our luggage
Or our reservations
Or two of the engines
Or the rinse that was going to give my hair some subtle copper
    highlights turned it purple
Or my mother-in-law got insulted at something I said
Or my stomach got upset at something I ate
Or I backed into a truck that I swear when I looked in my
    rearview mirror wasn't parked there
Or I suffered from some other blow of fate,
It's always been so nice to have my husband by my side so I could
Blame him.

MID-LIFE CRISIS

What am I doing with a mid-life crisis?
This morning I was seventeen.
I have barely begun the beguine and it's
Good night ladies
Already.

While I've been wondering who to be
When I grow up someday.
My acne has vanished away and it's
Sagging kneecaps
Already.

Why do I seem to remember Pearl Harbor?
Surely I must be too young.
When did the boys I once clung to
Start losing their hair?
Why can't I take barefoot walks in the park
Without giving my kidneys a chill?
There's poetry left in me still and it
Doesn't seem fair.

While I was thinking I was just a girl,
My future turned into my past.
The time for wild kisses goes fast and it's
Time for Sanka.
Already?

OPEN HOUSE

Everyone is coming to our party,
Everyone, that is, except the Stones,
Who stopped being the Stones when she started saying that
the trouble with America was the CIA and the FBI and
the exploitation of lettuce growers and Indians, and
He started saying the trouble was not enough tennis courts, but
Everyone else is coming to our party,
Everyone, that is, except the Hoyts,
Who stopped being the Hoyts when they started saying that just
because a husband and wife are sexually unfaithful doesn't
mean that they're being unfaithful emotionally, but
Everyone else is coming to our party,
Everyone, that is, except the Kings,
Who stopped being the Kings when she decided that every time she
told him something sensitive and deep he didn't get it, and
He decided that every time he told her something funny she didn't
get it, but
Everyone else is coming to our party,
Everyone, that is, except the Youngs,
Who stopped being the Youngs when she started law school,
And he started saying the house is never clean,
And she started saying why don't you clean it yourself,
And he started saying that women should clean and men should go
to law school, but
Everyone else is coming to our party,
Everyone, that is, except the Clarks,
Who stopped being the Clarks when she decided to seek inner peace
through wheat germ and meditation, and
He decided to seek inner peace through Gay Lib, but
Everyone else is coming to our party,
Everyone, that is, except the Greens,
Who stopped being the Greens when they sold their house and
moved to the country to rediscover each other, and rediscovered
they didn't agree about garlic. Or Woody Allen.
Or Scrabble, her father, cloth napkins, or psychoanalysis.
Or when is the music so loud that it's giving you headaches.
Or when is a room so ice-cold that your fingers get numb, but
Everyone else is coming to our party.
I hope we'll be there.

THREE IN
THE MORNING

At three in the morning I used to be sleeping an untroubled sleep
    in my bed,
But lately at three in the morning I'm tossing and turning,
Awakened by hypochondria, and gas, and nameless dread,
Whose name I've been learning.

At three in the morning I brood about what my cholesterol count
    might reveal,
And the pains in my chest start progressing from gentle to racking,
While certain intestinal problems make clear that the onions I
    ate with my meal
Plan on counterattacking.

At three in the morning I reach for the bottles of pills that I
    seem to possess
Increasingly larger amounts of as every year passes,
Except that I can't tell the ones for my nerves from the ones for
    my stomach distress
Till I put on my glasses.

At three in the morning I look toward the future with blankets
    pulled over my ears,
And all of my basic equipment distinctly diminished.
My gums are receding, my blood pressure's high, and I can't
    begin listing my fears
Or I'll never get finished.

At three in the morning I used to be sleeping but lately I wake
    and reflect
That my girlhood has gone and I'll now have to manage without it.
They tell me that I'm heading into my prime. From the previews
    I do not expect
To be crazy about it.

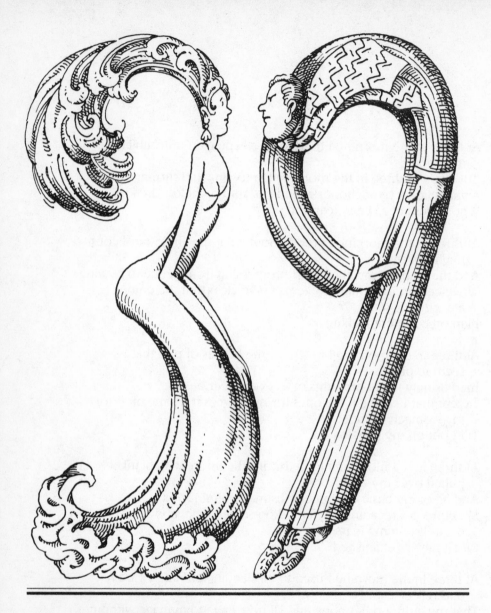

ALONE

Alone I could own both sides of the double bed
And stay up reading novels half the night.
And no one would be here telling me turn off the light
And hogging the blankets.

And no one would be here saying he's taking the car
And noticing that I let the milk turn sour.
Alone I could talk long distance for an hour
And who would stop me?

Alone a hard-boiled egg could be a meal
And the living-room couch could be red, not compromise-green.
And no one would be here making me go to Queens
For family brunches.

And no one would be here brushing his teeth with my brush
And pushing the thermostat down to sixty degrees.
Alone I could give Goodwill my boots and my skis
And switch to beaches.

Alone I could give up understanding Brie,
The Dow Jones average and his Cousin Rose.
And no one would be here telling me which of my clothes
Make me look chunky.

And no one would be here steaming the bathroom up
And wanting his back massaged and his buttons sewn.
And no one would be here. I would be alone
And I would hate it.

SELF~IMPROVEMENT PROGRAM

I've finished six pillows in Needlepoint,
And I'm reading Jane Austen and Kant,
And I'm up to the pork with black beans in Advanced Chinese Cooking.
I don't have to struggle to find myself
For I already know what I want.
I want to be healthy and wise and extremely good-looking.

I'm learning new glazes in Pottery Class,
And I'm playing new chords in Guitar,
And in Yoga I'm starting to master the lotus position.
I don't have to ponder priorities
For I already know what they are:
To be good-looking, healthy, and wise.
And adored in addition.

I'm improving my serve with a tennis pro,
And I'm practicing verb forms in Greek,
And in Primal Scream Therapy all my frustrations are vented.
I don't have to ask what I'm searching for
Since I already know that I seek
To be good-looking, healthy, and wise.
And adored.
And contented.

I've bloomed in Organic Gardening,
And in Dance I have tightened my thighs,
And in Consciousness Raising there's no one around who can top me.
And I'm working all day and I'm working all night
To be good-looking, healthy, and wise.
And adored.
And contented.
And brave.
And well-read.
And a marvelous hostess,
Fantastic in bed,
And bilingual,
Athletic,
Artistic . . .
Won't someone please stop me?

FAMILIARITY
BREEDS
CONTENT
(SONG OF THE LONG-MARRIED WOMAN)

Although our married life is full of strife, if you
    proposed again I'd grab it.
And while it's sometimes hard to be your wife, it's also
    quite a lovely habit.

Although our being wed has often led me to bemoan your
    imperfections,
It also seems that I have grown accustomed to your face,
    and other sections.

ADULT
EDUCATION

I have grown to understand that
People whose accents are British
May not be smarter than people whose accents are Bronx,
But British helps, and that
Peace of mind is more to be treasured than rubies,
But trust funds help, and that
While it's better to die on your feet than to live on your knees,
What about stooping?

I have grown to understand that
People whose best friends are rock stars
Often are duller than people whose best friends are us,
But rock stars help, and that
Inner satisfaction counts more than approval,
But clapping helps, and that
While it's better to light a candle than curse the darkness,
First you could curse.

I have grown to understand that
People whose fathers adored them
Feel just as jumpy as people whose fathers said feh,
But love helps, and that
Self-reliance is braver than being dependent,
But help helps, and that
While it's better, as everyone knows, to give than receive,
Nobody says that you always have to be
Better.

TWENTY
QUESTIONS

Can a person who used to wear a Ban the Bomb button
And a Free Angela Davis button
And an Uppity Women Unite button
And a Get Out of Viet Nam button
Find happiness being a person with a
Set of fondue forks, a fish poacher, and a wok?

Is there an economic rule that says
No matter how much we earn and how little we spend,
There's no such thing as getting out of hock?

How do I know if the time has come to
Accept my limitations,
Or whether I still ought to try to
Fulfill my promise?

How come I'm reading articles
With names like A Woman's Guide to Cosmetic Surgery
More than I'm reading the poems of Dylan Thomas?

If I had an either/or choice
Would I prefer to be deservedly respected,
Or would I prefer to be mindlessly adored?

If we totally take the blame when our children
Stutter and wet their beds,
And are busted and maladjusted and drop out of school,
Do we get to take the credit if our children
Grow up to be brilliant, plus very nice people,
Plus mentally healthy and chairmen of the board?

When, instead of vice versa,
Did I start to pick investments over adventure,
And clean over scenic, and comfortable over intense?

Why does a relationship
Between an older woman and younger man
Suddenly seem to make a lot of sense?

Why am I always dressed in styles
Which I swear, when they first come out,
Nothing on earth could possibly make me buy?

What are the things which,
Even though people won't be upset (they swear)
If I'll only admit,
I should always deny?

Are some human beings
Intellectually and emotionally incapable
Of ever reading a road map,
Or could I still learn to?

If six days a week I'm responsible
And self-sufficient and competent and mature,
On the seventh could I go find a womb to return to?

Couldn't a person who isn't expecting
Praise for what she's doing
At least expect some praise for not expecting it?

If I think that the fellow next door
Is attempting to give me a kiss in the kitchen,
Am I first allowed to be kissed before rejecting it?

How can I learn to relate to marijuana
And bisexuality
When I'm more at home with The Anniversary Waltz?

How come I've got these incredible insights
Into all of my faults,
And I've still got my faults?

Why couldn't somebody tell me
That I haven't changed since college
Without being practically blind or
A terrible liar?

Why, since I've never had any intention
Of going out on the street and selling my body,
Is it hard to be reaching an age where
I won't find a buyer?

How come a charter member of NOW
Is afraid to confess to her husband
That the first day she drove their new car
She dented the fender?

How will I ever be able to tell
If what I achieve in life
Ought to be called serenity—not surrender?

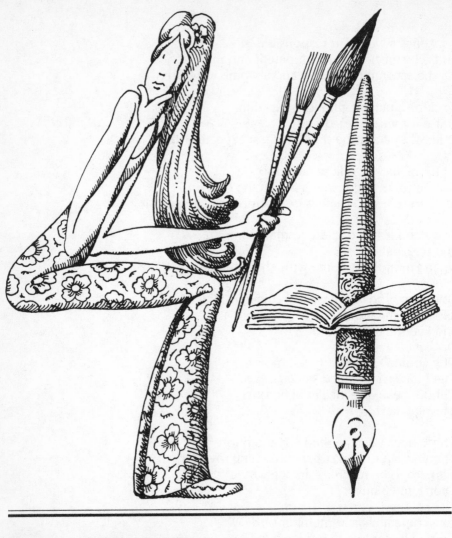

FACING
THE FACTS

I'm facing the fact that
I'll never write Dante's Inferno
Or paint a Picasso
Or transplant a kidney or build
An empire, nor will I ever
Run Israel or Harvard,
Appear on the cover of Time,
Star on Broadway, be killed
By a firing squad for some noble ideal,
Find the answer
To racial injustice or whether God's dead
Or the source
Of human unhappiness,
Alter the theories of Drs.
S. Freud, C. G. Jung, or A. Einstein,
Or maybe the course
Of history.
In addition to which
I am facing the fact that
I'll never compose Bach cantatas,
Design Saint Laurents,
Advise presidents, head U.S. Steel,
Resolve the Mideast,
Be the hostess of some major talk show,
Or cure the cold.
And although future years may reveal
Some hidden potential,
Some truly magnificent act that
I've yet to perform,
Or some glorious song to be sung,
For which I'll win prizes and praise,
I must still face the fact that
They'll never be able to say,
"And she did it so young."

About the Author

Judith Viorst is the author of ten collections of poetry, fifteen children's books, and nine other books. She lives in Washington, D.C., with her husband, Milton Viorst.